AF408413

Childlike Faith

By Ryonna Clark

Illustrated by Alissa Dicke

-To my parents

ISBN: 979-8-3481-8711-8

I know just what to do when I'm feeling sad.
I listen to my fathers words and they help me feel not
so bad.

I know just what to do when I can't make a choice...
my father guides me step by step while blocking out the noise.

I know just what to do when I'm feeling scared,
My father turns on all the lights and scares away all the
bears!

I know just what to do when I'm feeling small...

My father builds a tower and makes me super tall.

I know just what to do when I feel left out ...

My father brings friends, from North to South.

I know just what to do when I want to quit.
My father says " keep going child you're not finished yet!"

I know just what to do when I feel lost.
My father comes around and says "you're found!"

I know just what to do when I'm feeling sick.
My father brings me water and some medicine.

I know just what to do when I scrape my knee.
My father comes over and he bandages me.

I know just what to do when I've made a mistake.
My father says no worries tomorrow is a new day.

You see, I know just what to do in almost every situation because my father has given me every explanation.

He loves me and I love Him too, don't you know how much your Father loves you?

It's a simple thought and a simple quest, because the Father loves me just like He loves the rest.

I know this is true because He said it and there's no doubt in my heart that He meant it.

1 John 3:1 - "How great is the love the Father has lavished on us, that we should be called children of God! And that is what we are!"

Ryonna with her father

For your guidance, endless love,
support, and laughs. Thank you for
teaching me to put Christ first in all
that I do and for being my friend.